Technology Timelines

AIRCRAFT

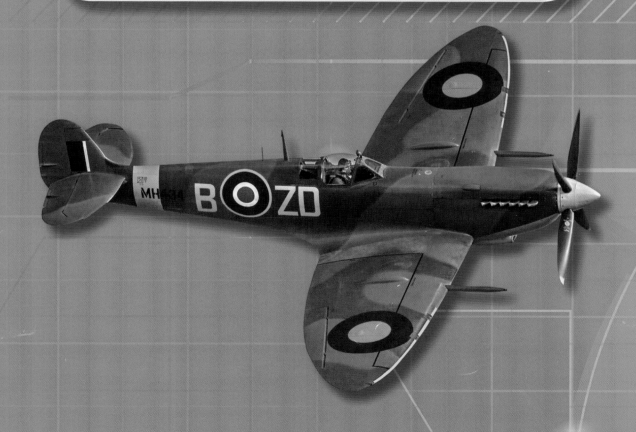

BROWN BEAR BOOKS

Published by Brown Bear Books Ltd

4877 N. Circulo Bujia
Tucson, AZ 85718
USA

and

First Floor
9-17 St. Albans Place
London N1 0NX

© 2015 Brown Bear Books Ltd

ISBN: 978-1-78121-236-3

Library of Congress Cataloging-in-Publication Data available upon request

Author: Tom Jackson
Designer: Lynne Lennon
Picture Researcher: Clare Newman
Children's Publisher: Anne O'Daly
Design Manager: Keith Davis
Editorial Director: Lindsey Lowe

Manufactured in the United States of America

CPSIA compliance information: Batch# AG/5568

Contents

Introduction

The first airplane took flight about one hundred years ago. It had taken many centuries for people to learn to fly. In the 1000s, Eilmer, an English monk, jumped off an abbey in Wiltshire, England, equipped with a set of wood and cloth wings. He glided a little way but then fell and broke both his legs. Since then, many more brave people have risked their lives to achieve the power of flight.

Aerial Carriage

Early flying machines had flapping wings, like birds. The fixed wing was developed by Englishman George Cayley. His aerial carriage of 1843 had four disks that were designed to raise the machine vertically. In 1853, he built a glider that could carry a person.

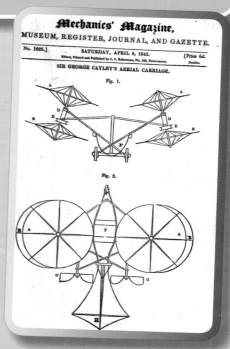

The First Aircraft

A hot-air balloon was the first flying machine. After testing fabric and paper balloons with animal passengers, the French Montgolfier brothers built one big enough to lift a crew of two people. It made its first flight over Paris in 1783.

CREATING LIFT

An airplane rises into the air because its wings create a lift force. This is because of the wing's "airfoil" shape, with a flat bottom but curved upper surface. Air rushing over the top travels faster and farther than the air passing underneath. This means that the air pressure above the wing is lower than below it. The difference in pressure creates the upward lift force.

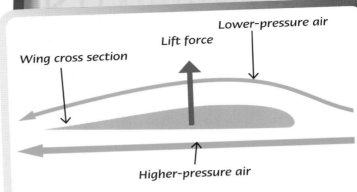

Lift force

Lower-pressure air

Wing cross section

Higher-pressure air

As the angle of the wing increases, the lift force also goes up. This is because there is a greater difference between the air pressures above and below the wing.

Lighter than Air

Hydrogen gas is so light that it floats up through the air. This hydrogen balloon was used for spying on the enemy in the American Civil War in the 1860s. These balloons inspired the invention of the airship, the first long-distance passenger aircraft, which also used hydrogen gas.

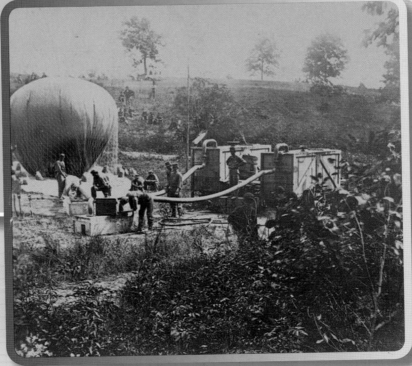

Taking to the Air

The first motorized airplane flew in December, 1903, from a beach near Kitty Hawk, North Carolina. It was flown by the brothers Orville and Wilbur Wright.

Before the Wright brothers, many early aviators had built simple aircraft big enough to carry a person. However, they were just gliders. None of them had engines—adding one made them too heavy to fly. The big breakthrough from the Wright brothers was a small gasoline-driven engine that was light but still powerful enough to lift their aircraft.

Wright Flyer I

History records this as the first real airplane. As well as having an engine, the pilot could steer it in any direction when in flight.

THE WOODEN PROPELLERS were at the back of the aircraft. They were attached to the engine by bicycle chains.

THE RUDDER at the back turned Flyer I from side to side.

THE LIGHTWEIGHT ENGINE was powered by gasoline.

TIMELINE

1890
Steam Plane
Frenchman Clément Ader flies his steam-powered machine, *Éole* (right), for 160 feet (50 m) near Paris.

1892
Wright Cycle Company
Orville and Wilbur Wright start making bicycles in Dayton, Ohio.

1904
Round Trip
Orville Wright takes *Wright Flyer II* on the first circular flight, successfully turning the plane around in the air and landing.

THE PILOT lay on his stomach. He steered by pulling on wires to warp, or change the shape of, the wings.

THE WINGS were made from muslin, a thin cotton fabric, stretched over a wooden frame.

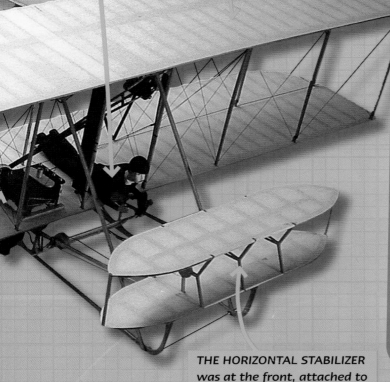

THE HORIZONTAL STABILIZER was at the front, attached to the skids.

OTTO LILIENTHAL

The fixed-wing gliders of German aviator Otto Lilienthal were a great inspiration to the Wright brothers. Lilienthal leaped off hills to catch the wind and rise into the air. In 1896, he broke his neck in a fatal crash.

« POWER PEOPLE »

1908
Airwoman
Thérèse Peltier, a French artist, is the first woman to fly in an airplane and to take the controls on a solo flight.

1909
Monoplane
French aviator Louis Blériot makes the first flight across the English Channel. He uses the first working monoplane, an aircraft with one fixed wing.

Dogfighters

Many of the first aircraft were built for the military. They were originally used for collecting information about enemy forces on the ground, but they soon became a new form of weapon.

THE UPPER MACHINE GUN *could be used to fire upward as well as forward.*

The first attack aircraft were bombers, which were powerful airplanes that could carry heavy explosives and drop them on targets. To defend against bombers, small and fast "fighters" were developed to shoot them down. The first air battles, or "dogfights," occurred in World War I (1914–1918).

THE FUSELAGE *had a wooden frame and was covered in fabric.*

Royal Aircraft Factory S.E.5

The S.E.5 was a fighter used by the British Royal Flying Corps (later, Royal Air Force, or RAF) in World War I. The aircraft had two guns, carried four bombs, and flew 138 miles per hour (222 km/h).

THE RUDDER *and other steering flaps were connected to the cockpit controls by tight wires.*

TIMELINE

1911
Land and Sea
U.S. flier Glenn Curtiss builds a seaplane with floats and wheels that can operate from both water and dry land.

1916
First Boeing
William E. Boeing test flies the B&W Seaplane, (also known as Boeing Model 1), the first of many aircraft from the U.S. Boeing company.

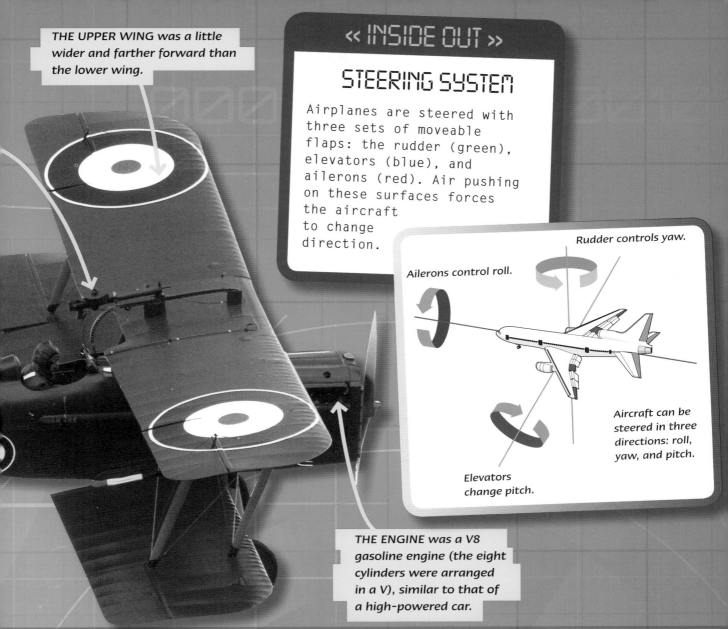

THE UPPER WING was a little wider and farther forward than the lower wing.

STEERING SYSTEM

Airplanes are steered with three sets of moveable flaps: the rudder (green), elevators (blue), and ailerons (red). Air pushing on these surfaces forces the aircraft to change direction.

Rudder controls yaw.

Ailerons control roll.

Aircraft can be steered in three directions: roll, yaw, and pitch.

Elevators change pitch.

THE ENGINE was a V8 gasoline engine (the eight cylinders were arranged in a V), similar to that of a high-powered car.

1919

Transatlantic Flight

Two British pilots, John Alcock and Arthur Brown, fly a two-engined Vickers Vimy bomber nonstop across the Atlantic from Ireland to Canada.

60f

1920

Airmail

The first U.S. airborne mail service carries letters from New York to San Francisco in 33 hours—almost three days faster than sending them by train.

Lighter than Air

Early airplanes could not fly very far and only had room for a few passengers. The first passenger aircraft were not airplanes, but giant airships. These gas balloons could fly for hours, carrying passengers in great comfort.

Large airships, also called zeppelins for their German inventor, Ferdinand von Zeppelin, were first tested in 1900. Zeppelins were filled with hydrogen and floated in the air in the same way that dry wood floats in water. The gas balloons were housed inside a sleek outer frame.

Passenger Airship

By the 1920s, there were regular airship services across the Atlantic. Zeppelins went to the North Pole and even flew all the way around the world.

HUGE BAGS inside the frame were filled with hydrogen gas, which is much lighter than the surrounding air. However, a tiny spark could cause the gas to explode at any time.

A METAL FRAME gave the airship its rigid shape.

FINS on the tail kept the airship flying straight and level.

TIMELINE

1923
Autogiro
The first autogiro (below), an airplane using a free-spinning rotor instead of a fixed wing, flies in Spain.

1924
Around the World
Two aircraft land in Seattle, Washington, after a 175-day journey around the world, made in 74 flights.

1925
Inflight Movie
On an Imperial Airways flight from London to Paris, a silent movie, *The Lost World*, is shown to passengers.

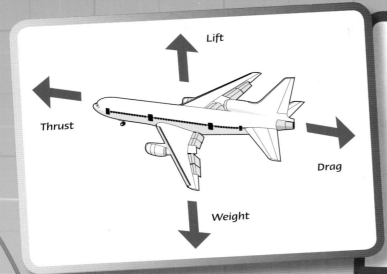

Lift

Thrust

Drag

Weight

THE FOUR FORCES

A flying machine has four forces acting on it. To get off the ground, the upward lift force must be greater than the weight (or pull of gravity). To move forward, the thrust produced by the aircraft's engines must be greater than the drag, or the force of the air pushing back on the aircraft.

« INSIDE OUT »

PROPELLER ENGINES on either side produced thrust. The pilot steered by varying the power applied to either side.

THE CABINS for pilot and passengers were located underneath the airship.

A CATWALK running through the center let the crew inspect the gas bags during flights.

A FABRIC ENVELOPE covered the airship, making it sleek and aerodynamic.

1927

Solo Flight

U.S. aviator Charles Lindbergh makes the first solo flight over the Atlantic Ocean, flying from New York to Paris, France.

1929

Instrument Flight

U.S. pilot Jimmy Doolittle flies using only cockpit instruments (he could not see the ground). Doolittle then develops the "artificial horizon," which shows the position of the plane.

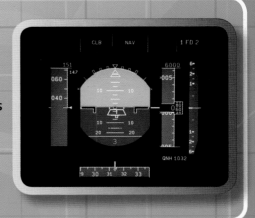

Long Distance

As engines became more powerful and reliable, aircraft journeys became more common. However, there were not many runways, so planes that made long journeys were designed to land on water.

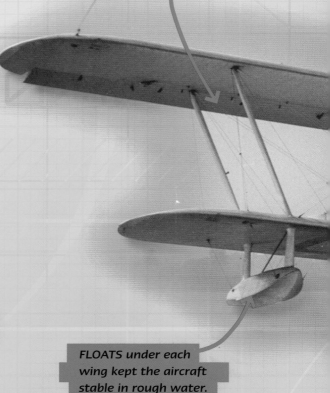

THE UPPER WING was about the height of a two-story house.

A flying boat is an aircraft with a fuselage shaped like a ship's hull. It can land on rivers, lakes, and the sea, as long as the water is calm. In the 1930s, the rich and famous traveled the world in these aircraft. Long journeys were made in several short hops. It took 16 days to fly from Great Britain to Australia—more than twice as fast as a ship.

Short Calcutta

This British flying boat could fly more than 620 miles (1,000 km) at one time. It was used on services in the Mediterranean Sea and Indian Ocean in the 1930s.

FLOATS under each wing kept the aircraft stable in rough water.

TIMELINE

1930

Jet Engine
Frank Whittle, a British RAF test pilot, designs the first jet engine, but he cannot get funding to develop the technology.

1933

The 247
The all-metal Boeing 247 (right) is the first airliner to have retractable wheels and an autopilot system. A total of 75 are built.

THE THREE ENGINES were fitted between the wings and high above the water.

TWO PILOTS sat in an open-air cockpit.

THE BOAT-SHAPED HULL was made from stretched aluminum, making it light but strong.

THE CABIN had room for 15 passengers and a steward.

1934
Mother Ship
Small Sparrowhawk fighters launch in midair from a U.S. military airship. They then hook back onto the airship while it is still flying.

1936
The Dakota
The DC-3 airliner becomes the most successful early airliner. The military version is called the Dakota.

1937
Hindenburg Crash
The German airship *Hindenburg*, which was filled with hydrogen, explodes while landing in New Jersey, killing 36 people.

War in the Air

World War II led to many advances in aviation technology. This was the time when the first jet and rocket-powered airplanes were developed. However, most aircraft were still powered by propellers.

Air power was a crucial factor in World War II. The side that controlled the airspace above a battlefield would win on the ground as well. More than 830,000 airplanes took part in the fighting.

Supermarine Spitfire

This famous British fighter was designed to fly fast to intercept enemy bombers. It was very effective during the Battle of Britain in 1940. It was also very maneuverable, so it could twist and turn during midair battles.

A MAST connects a wire radio aerial to the tail.

THE FUEL TANK was positioned between the cockpit and the engine.

THE FUSELAGE was a long tube of aluminum plates bolted around 19 metal rings of different sizes.

THE WHEELS, or undercarriage, fold into a space under the wing when the fighter is flying.

TIMELINE

1939

First Jet Fighter
The Heinkel He 178 designed by German Hans von Ohain is the first jet-powered aircraft to fly.

1942

The Flying Bomb
The V-1 "doodlebug," a pilotless jet-powered bomb, has its first flight in Germany. In 1944, it is used to attack England and Belgium.

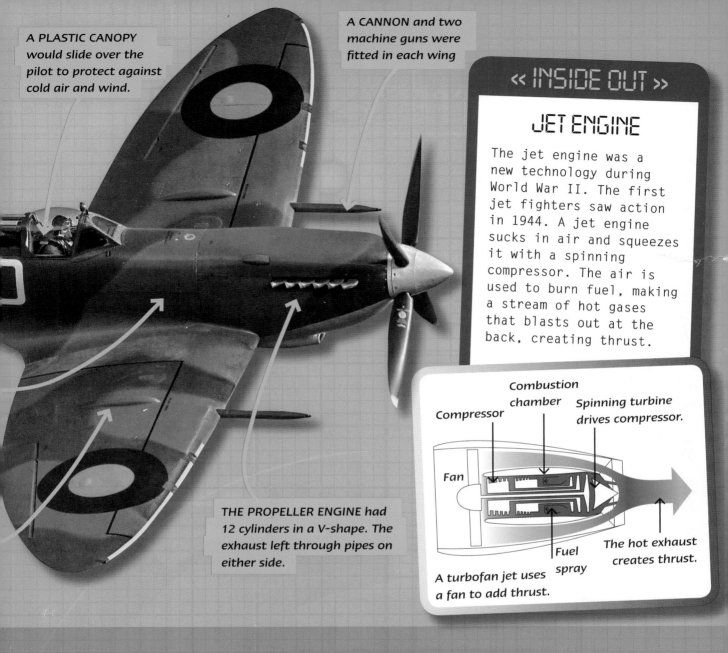

A PLASTIC CANOPY would slide over the pilot to protect against cold air and wind.

A CANNON and two machine guns were fitted in each wing

JET ENGINE

The jet engine was a new technology during World War II. The first jet fighters saw action in 1944. A jet engine sucks in air and squeezes it with a spinning compressor. The air is used to burn fuel, making a stream of hot gases that blasts out at the back, creating thrust.

Compressor

Combustion chamber

Spinning turbine drives compressor.

Fan

Fuel spray

The hot exhaust creates thrust.

A turbofan jet uses a fan to add thrust.

THE PROPELLER ENGINE had 12 cylinders in a V-shape. The exhaust left through pipes on either side.

1944

Rocket Plane

The Messerschmitt Me 163 Komet, used by the German Air Force, is the first (and only) rocket-powered fighter aircraft.

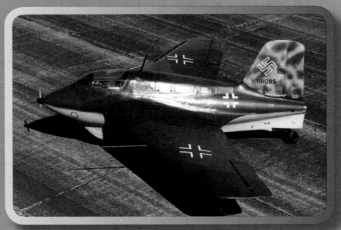

1946

Explosive Ejector

Ejector seats that fire pilots to safety out of the cockpit using rockets are tested with real people for the first time.

The X Planes

In the late 1940s, the world's engineers began to try out new types of aircraft. In the United States, the experimental aircraft are called X planes, and X–1 was the first aircraft to fly faster than sound.

In 1947, the American test pilot Chuck Yeager became the first person to fly faster than the speed of sound. No one knew what would happen to a person moving that fast or whether an aircraft could still fly. Bullets fired from most guns break the sound barrier but still travel in straight lines. Therefore, the X-1 was shaped like a bullet.

Bell X-I

Made by the Bell company, the X-1 completed 157 flights between 1946 and 1951. It achieved a top speed of 957 miles per hour (1,540 km/h) in 1948.

THE TINY COCKPIT had no ejector seat. The pilot had to land to survive the flight.

THE NOSE CONE was shaped like a bullet, so that it could power through the sound barrier.

THE WINGS were very thin to reduce drag at high speed. They were also very stiff, so that the plane flew straight at high speeds.

TIMELINE

1949

Lucky Lady II
A U.S. B-50 Superfortress bomber flies around the world without landing. The aircraft flew for 94 hours and was refueled in midair four times.

1955

Vertijet
The X-13 experimental aircraft is designed to operate without a runway. It takes off and lands vertically—and can hover in midair.

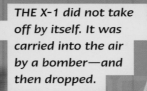

THE X-1 did not take off by itself. It was carried into the air by a bomber—and then dropped.

THE ROCKET blasted out of a nozzle under the tail.

6062

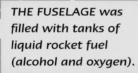

THE FUSELAGE was filled with tanks of liquid rocket fuel (alcohol and oxygen).

« INSIDE OUT »

SUPERSONIC

Sounds are pressure waves traveling through the air. The waves travel at a fixed speed—around 700 miles per hour (1,125 km/h). Speeds below this are subsonic; to go faster is to be supersonic.

1. At subsonic speeds, sound waves spread out from the plane in all directions.

Sound wave

2. At the speed of sound, the sound waves build up into a shock wave.

Shock wave

3. At supersonic speeds, the shock wave forms a cone, which creates a loud sonic boom.

Cone

Sonic boom heard on the ground.

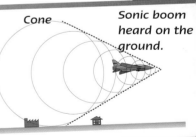

1956

Small Aircraft

The Cessna 172 small aircraft is introduced. Since then, about 42,000 of these planes have been built, more than any other model of aircraft.

1959

X-15 Spaceplane

The first flights of the rocket-powered X-15 are made. The plane is able to reach the edge of space and fly at six times the speed of sound.

Airliners

During the 1960s, air travel became more popular as jet-powered airliners made long journeys faster and safer than ever before. Where once people had traveled on ocean liners, they began to fly instead.

The airliner has been around for almost as long as the airplane. However, by the 1960s, they were large enough to carry hundreds of passengers, which made each ticket much less expensive. Traveling at almost the speed of sound, airliners took hours to make journeys that had previously taken days.

Boeing 747 "Jumbo"

The 747 is one of the most famous airliners. It is a "wide-body," with room for ten seats in each row. A "narrow-body" has six seats across.

FOUR ENGINES hang from the wings. The aircraft can fly safely for a short distance with just one engine.

FLAPS extend to make the wing bigger, allowing the airplane to fly safely at slower speeds.

THE FLIGHT DECK is accessible only to the pilots and other crew members.

THE GALLEY is the aircraft's kitchen.

TIMELINE

1960

U-2 Incident

A U.S. U-2 spy plane, designed to fly too high to be shot down, is shot down over Russia (then the Soviet Union). Later U.S. spy planes are built to be so fast they can outrun any attacker.

1966

Blackbird

The SR-71 Blackbird (below), the fastest jet aircraft, enters service as a spy plane.

1969

Jump Jet

The Harrier fighter has jets that can direct thrust down as well as backward. This allows it to hover and to take off and land vertically.

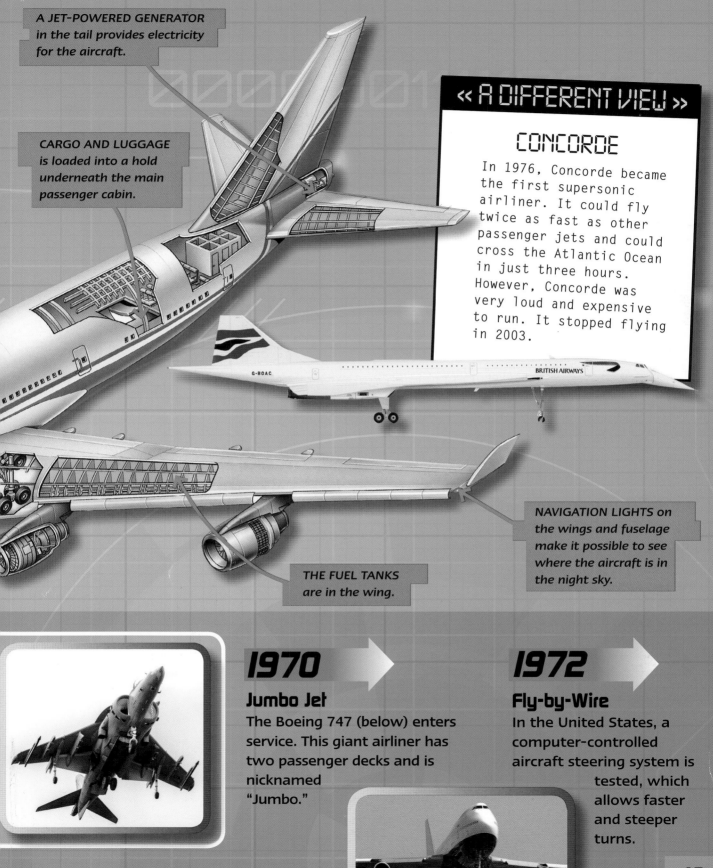

A JET-POWERED GENERATOR in the tail provides electricity for the aircraft.

CARGO AND LUGGAGE is loaded into a hold underneath the main passenger cabin.

« A DIFFERENT VIEW »

CONCORDE

In 1976, Concorde became the first supersonic airliner. It could fly twice as fast as other passenger jets and could cross the Atlantic Ocean in just three hours. However, Concorde was very loud and expensive to run. It stopped flying in 2003.

G-BOAC

BRITISH AIRWAYS

NAVIGATION LIGHTS on the wings and fuselage make it possible to see where the aircraft is in the night sky.

THE FUEL TANKS are in the wing.

1970

Jumbo Jet

The Boeing 747 (below) enters service. This giant airliner has two passenger decks and is nicknamed "Jumbo."

1972

Fly-by-Wire

In the United States, a computer-controlled aircraft steering system is tested, which allows faster and steeper turns.

Fast Jets

By the 1970s, a fighter jet had to have a wide range of capabilities: It had to be supersonic to outrun the enemy, but it also had to be highly maneuverable in dogfights.

The next generation of fighter aircraft used fly-by-wire. This means that the control surfaces (the rudder, elevators, and ailerons) were not controlled directly by the pilot. Instead, a computer adjusted them constantly to keep the plane stable—and let the pilot steer when he or she wanted to. This made it possible for aircraft to have a pointed, supersonic shape but also to make fast turns without losing lift.

Panavia Tornado

Introduced to European air forces in 1979, the Tornado is a fighter-bomber designed to defend against air attacks and to bomb enemy targets.

A RADAR DETECTOR on the tail warns the crew when the aircraft has been picked up by enemy radar.

FUEL TANKS are added to the wings for long flights.

THE WINGS stick out sideways for slow flight but swing back for supersonic speeds.

TIMELINE

1977

World's Worst Crash

Two jumbo jets crash into each other during takeoff from Tenerife, Canary Islands, killing 583 people. Strict new rules for air traffic control are introduced to boost safety.

1979

Gossamer Albatross

The first human-powered aircraft flies across the English Channel. The pilot spins the propeller with a cycle mechanism.

AIR INTAKES on either side suck in the air needed to burn the engine fuel.

THE COCKPIT has room for a crew of two. The pilot sits in front of the navigator.

ELECTRONICS in the nose cone detect enemy aircraft and targets on the ground.

MISSILES AND BOMBS are hung under the fuselage.

« INSIDE OUT »

WING SHAPES

The shapes of airplane wings vary depending on what they are designed to do and how fast they can fly. If an airplane flies too slowly, it will "stall"—the wings won't create enough lift.

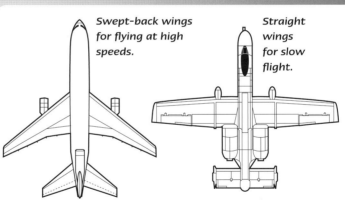

Swept-back wings for flying at high speeds.

Straight wings for slow flight.

"Swing-wings" allow fighters to fly at a range of speeds.

Forward

Back

1981

Space Plane

The space shuttle *Columbia* (right) is launched into space and later glides back to Earth, becoming the first reusable spacecraft.

1983

Stealth Fighter

The F-117 Nighthawk is introduced by the U.S. Air Force. It is the first "stealth" aircraft, designed to be invisible to radars and other detectors.

Top Secret

To combat fast jets, military radar was developed that could see them coming—and fire off high-speed missiles in defense. What was needed was an aircraft that was invisible to radar.

A stealth plane is one that can fly over enemy territory without being detected. The first stealth planes were developed in the 1980s and were kept top secret.

B-2 Spirit

Also known as the Stealth Bomber, the B-2 was introduced in 1997. It has never been fired on during combat, although it is thought that the most advanced radar systems can now detect it.

THE FLYING WING shape has no tail. The bomber is steered by a series of flaps running along its zigzagged wing.

THE HOT ENGINES are hidden inside the aircraft, so that heat-seeking missiles cannot detect them.

INSTEAD OF METAL, the bomber is made of light but super-strong carbon fibers.

THE BOMBER is more than 170 feet (52 m) wide and flies very high to stay out of sight.

TIMELINE

1986
Nonstop Flight
The Rutan Voyager takes nine days to fly all the way around the world—24,987 miles (40,212 km)—on a single tank of fuel.

1990s
Cruise Missile
Flying bombs are developed that are powered by small jet engines and able to navigate to a target by themselves.

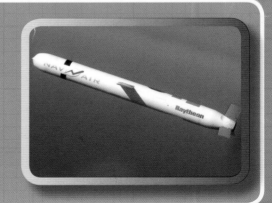

BREITLING ORBITER 3

In 1999, 213 years after the first manned balloon flight, a hot-air balloon managed to fly nonstop around the planet. With a crew of two, it took 19 days for the *Breitling Orbiter 3* (which also had helium-filled sections) to make the flight.

« A DIFFERENT VIEW »

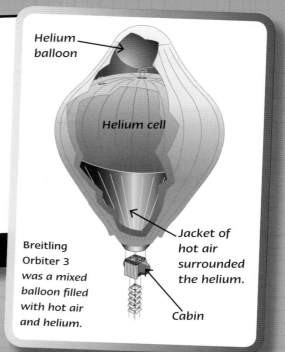

Helium balloon

Helium cell

Jacket of hot air surrounded the helium.

Cabin

Breitling Orbiter 3 was a mixed balloon filled with hot air and helium.

THE HOT EXHAUST GAS *is spread out into a thin plume by the engine to make it harder to detect.*

THE BLACK SKIN *absorbs radio waves and heat, so that the airplane does not show up on detection systems.*

1994
Youngest Pilot
Twelve-year-old American Vicki van Meter becomes the youngest pilot to fly across the Atlantic Ocean.

1997
Airbus Beluga
A giant transport plane is designed by the Airbus company to carry aircraft parts (left).

AIRBUS Think Mobil 3

2001
Solar Power
The NASA Helios, an unmanned solar-powered plane, flies to 96,863 feet (29,524 m), the highest altitude of any powered aircraft.

Drones

Some aircraft can fly without a pilot on board. They are called drones, or unmanned aerial vehicles, and are controlled via satellite by a human on the ground—often in another country.

THE V-SHAPED TAIL does not interfere with the engine and reduces the noise it makes.

A drone does not get tired and can stay in the air for long periods—being refueled when needed by other aircraft, even other drones! They can also go to places that are too risky for humans to go to. Even if the drone is attacked, the remote pilot stays safe.

THE LONG WINGS mean that the aircraft can fly slowly at high altitudes for several hours at a time.

MQ-9 Reaper

The Reaper drone has been used by the U.S. military since 2007. It has a powerful camera that is used to watch what is happening on the ground. The drones are also used to attack targets.

MISSILES are attached to the wing. The pilot can launch attacks by remote control.

TIMELINE

2004

Hyper Speed

The X-43 reaches 7,000 mph (10,460 km/h) using a combination of a rocket booster and an experimental engine called a scramjet.

2004

SpaceShipOne

A rocket plane is the first craft to fly into space twice in two weeks. It takes off under a jet aircraft (right) before blasting up into space.

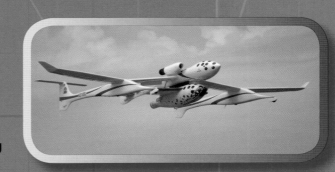

> **A TURBOPROP ENGINE** is at the back. In this engine, a jet turbine is used to spin a propeller.

> **INSTEAD OF A CREW,** the aircraft carries around 450 lb. (200 kg) of computers.

> **A POWERFUL CAMERA** can look in all directions to show the pilot what is in the area.

GLASS COCKPIT

Instead of having dials and switches, a modern aircraft cockpit, like this one from an Airbus, has computer screens and keyboards. A drone pilot uses this kind of "glass cockpit." He or she does not look through a windshield—they see the surroundings on a screen.

« A DIFFERENT VIEW »

2005

Super Jumbo

The A380, a huge double-decker airliner, takes to the air. The plane can carry 853 people a third of the way around the world.

2010

Volcanic Cloud

Ash from a volcano in Iceland spreads over Europe. It forces all airliners to stay on the ground for six days, since the ash can damage jet engines.

Speed and Stealth

The age of human fliers is far from over. The latest fighter jets are the F-35s. These aircraft can fly at supersonic speeds, use stealth to avoid detection, and one type can even land without a runway.

The F-35 Lightning II, also known as the Joint Strike Fighter, is being built by several countries, and is designed to replace several older types of aircraft because it can do so many different things. It will not be finished for a few years, and each aircraft will cost $190 million! The plane is a flying supercomputer. The pilot's helmet visor is a screen that adds layers of information to what the pilots can see out of the cockpit with their own eyes.

FUEL TANKS *are fitted into the tail fins and wings.*

A FAN behind the cockpit is used to create a downward thrust, so the fighter can move vertically.

THE PILOT *controls the aircraft using voice commands.*

THE JETMAN

Yves Rossy is a Swiss aviator who flies using a jet-powered wing suit. He travels into the air aboard a larger aircraft and then jumps out, starting his engines as he falls. To land, he turns off the jets and parachutes to the ground.

<< POWER PEOPLE >>

TILT ROTOR

The Osprey has two huge propellers that can tilt up to work like a helicopter or swing to the front to power forward flight. The Osprey can fly faster and carry more cargo than a helicopter, but it does not need an airport to land.

« A DIFFERENT VIEW »

1. The aircraft's rotors point upward for a vertical takeoff.

2. Once in the air, the pilot swivels the rotors around.

3. The rotors are positioned at the tips of wings, and when they are facing forward, the Osprey flies forward like other aircraft.

DOORS cover the fan when it is not in use.

THE JET NOZZLE can be pointed downward for vertical takeoff and landing.

A STEALTH COATING makes the fighter difficult to detect with a radar.

THE AVIONICS, short for "aviation electronics," are stored along the side.

SLATS extend from the front of the wings to help it fly at slower speeds.

27

The Future of Flight

There are many ways that aircraft may develop in the future. They could become so fast that flights to the other side of the world will only take a couple of hours. The airliners we take on vacation will become larger and more comfortable—and there may be planes that never have to land.

« A DIFFERENT VIEW »

BIOFUELS

Aircraft fuel is a major source of carbon dioxide gas, which is linked with climate problems. In the future, air fuel may be made from the oily seeds of jatropha, a desert shrub.

See-Through Cabin

Aircraft are not made from metal anymore but a mix of materials. In the future, the skin of an aircraft may be see-through, so you get a fantastic view during your journey.

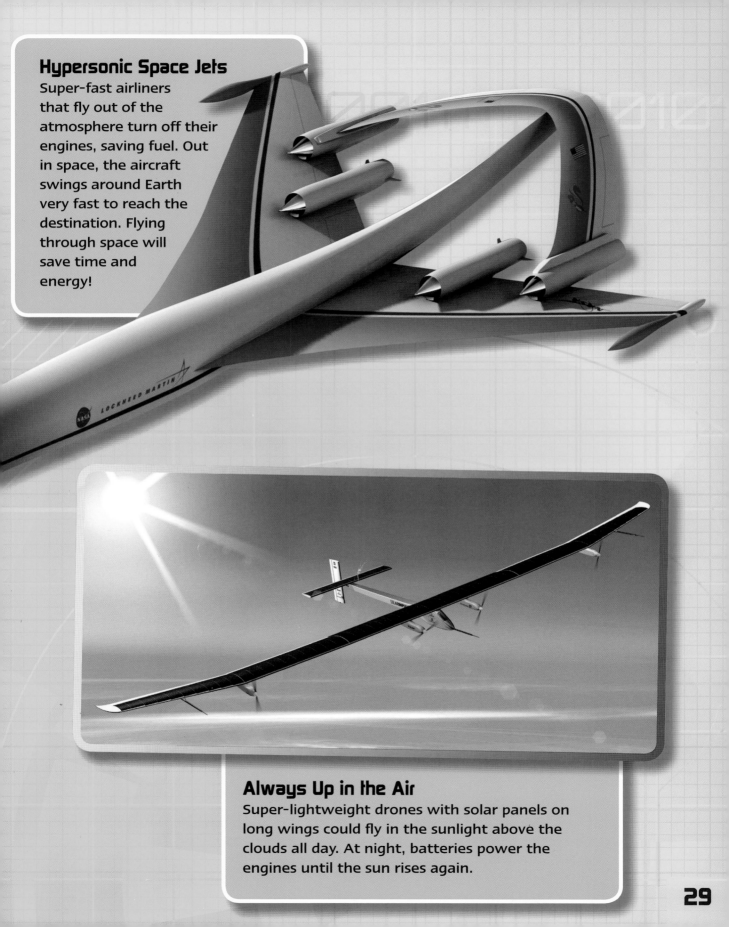

Hypersonic Space Jets

Super-fast airliners that fly out of the atmosphere turn off their engines, saving fuel. Out in space, the aircraft swings around Earth very fast to reach the destination. Flying through space will save time and energy!

Always Up in the Air

Super-lightweight drones with solar panels on long wings could fly in the sunlight above the clouds all day. At night, batteries power the engines until the sun rises again.

Glossary

aerial From or in the air.

airfoil A shape that creates a lift force when air rushes around it.

air pressure A force applied by air on the surface of a solid.

altitude Height above the ground.

artificial horizon A cockpit indicator that shows the pilot how the aircraft is positioned in relation to the horizon.

fuselage The main body of an aircraft containing the cabin and hold.

glider An aircraft that flies without an engine.

helium A safe, lightweight gas used in modern balloons and airships.

horizontal stabilizer Small wings that keep the airplane level. They are normally at the back of the aircraft but can be positioned at the front.

hydrogen The most lightweight gas of all, meaning it can carry balloons and airships higher than other gases or hot air, but it is highly flammable.

hypersonic A speed that is more than five times faster than sound.

pitch A motion that makes an aircraft's nose rise and fall. Pitch is controlled by elevators on the tail.

radar A detection system that bounces radio waves off distant objects and can calculate their location, speed, and size from the echo.

roll A motion that makes one wing tip rise and the other drop. Roll is controlled by ailerons on the wing.

rotor An airfoil that spins around.

turbine A fanlike system used in jet engines that converts a stream of gas into a spinning motion.

turbofan A jet engine that uses a fan to increase thrust.

turboprop A propeller engine powered by a jet turbine.

undercarriage The wheels, skids, or floats that the aircraft stands on.

yaw A motion where the aircraft nose moves one way and the tail, the other. Yaw is controlled by the rudder.

Further Resources

Books

Allen, Kenny. *Aircraft Carriers* (Monster Machines!). New York: Gareth Stevens Publishing, 2014.

Carson, Mary Kay. *The Wright Brothers for Kids: How They Invented the Airplane, 21 Activities Exploring the Science and History of Flight*. Chicago: Chicago Review Press, 2003.

Graham, Ian. *How Machines Work: Aircraft*. Mankato, MN: Smart Apple Media, 2008.

Nahum, Andrew. *Flight* (DK Eyewitness Books). New York: Dorling Kindersley, 2011.

Solway, Andrew. *Aircraft* (Sci-Hi: Science and Technology). Chicago: Heinemann-Raintree, 2011.

Websites

science.howstuffworks.com/ transport/flight/modern/airplanes. htm
Learn the basics of flight and aircraft design from HowStuffWorks.

www.airbus.com/innovation/ future-by-airbus/
Discover the future of aircraft according to Airbus.

www.boeing.com/boeing/history/ chronology/chron01.page
Search this interactive timeline from the Boeing company.

www.gefs-online.com/gefs.php#
Try your hand at flying a range of aircraft with this simulator. You can choose to fly anywhere on Earth and even fly over your own house.

www.nasa.gov/centers/ armstrong/history/index.html
Find out about NASA's X planes and experimental aircraft.

www.pbs.org/wgbh/nova/wright/
Check out this site filled with information about the Wright brothers and their aircraft.

Index